GLASGOW
FRAME *by* FRAME

D1578769

WELCOME to Glasgow: Frame by Frame, an 84-page publication crammed full of evocative and real-life images of a time that many of us will remember with equal measures of fondness and fascination.

Images of a city that evolved from a small sixth-century town into a sprawling metropolis.

But this journal is far more than a mere historical record of a famous city – it represents who we are, where we came from and how we lived.

We've delved deep into the picture archives at the Daily Record and Sunday Mail to bring you moving, witty and sombre images that document daily life in Scotland's biggest and most vibrant city.

Included in these pages are more than 200 stunning images of people, places and pastimes.

Memories of the wartime spirit that galvanised a suffering city, of the times when people power helped improve conditions for the working man and also the dark days of gang culture.

Children at play and a glimpse of our stunning architecture are also captured in atmospheric black and white.

Did you grow up in an era when Glasgow really did seem like the dance capital of the world? Were you part of a family that called a tenement block "home"? And were you "invited" to live the high-rise dream?

We also take a look at Glasgow's future, with the staging of the 2014 Commonwealth Games edging ever closer.

Whatever your background, if you're a son or daughter of Glasgow then this magazine is for you.

Editor: Jeff Holmes

Picture Reseach: Brian Gallagher, Ann-Marie Nimmo

Design & Production: Ewan Lauder

Marketing & Circulation: Debbie Ramsay, Tom Heffernan

©2012 Trinity Mirror / Daily Record & Sunday Mail Ltd. All rights reserved.

ISBN 0-9544202-7-6

Imagination
Children from the slums in the
Dalmarnock Road district used
any materials that came to
hand to play their games. Even
an old dustbin came in useful

Always something to do in the back courts

In the days before games consoles, children made their own entertainment – and it lasted from dawn until dusk

GLASWEGIANS of a certain vintage will vividly recall the days when children played outdoors from dawn until dusk.

A mother's shout from an open window "Are ye hungry?" was often met with the reply "Jist fling me doon a piece, mammy!"

A jam sandwich was duly despatched from a second-floor tenement window. Sometimes, it might be tucked safely inside a brown paper bag procured from the corner shop. But it would normally fly unprotected through the air – and whether or not its intended target managed to catch it was immaterial.

The grubby paws awaiting the tasty "treat" probably hadn't seen soap and water for a few hours anyway, so it was no big deal if it did hit the ground. Bacteria and viruses were of no concern to these kids.

But that was Glasgow tenement life. There were no rules in the back court play areas where children spent the bulk of their time. No day excursions to the museum or cafe on Byres Road for 60s and 70s kids.

Daybreak until nightfall was spent playing peever, tig or a myriad of other contemporary games.

Kids learned to improvise from an early age – utilising whatever could be found, be it an old tyre, tin bath or length of rope that was easily converted into a swing.

Many youngsters "raked the middens" for "luckies", or, to put it another way, checked to see what

▲ Upsy daisy
A youth worker plays with children against the backdrop of a Gorbals slum tenement development in January 1966

others, perhaps slightly better-off, had dumped in their rubbish bins.

Parents, knowing everyone looked out for each other's kids, were content to see their offspring happily spending the bulk of the school holidays running around unsupervised from day to day. No computer games or an endless supply of DVDs to watch.

You made your own entertainment and, if fortunate enough, a couple of "ginger" bottles would come your way – allowing you to march to the corner shop and exchange them for sweets. Nothing extravagant, just a toffee "frying pan" or penny dainty.

Then it was back out to play until the first patches of darkness began to fill the early evening sky.

▼ Street games This dedicated 'play street' was a safe haven for kids in Shettleston in 1958

Thirsty work This little girl decided to have a drink from the well at the Botanic Gardens in the west end during a trip there in March, 1948

◄ Revolution A group of schoolgirls enjoy a shot on the roundabout in leafy Queen's Park

▲ Playmobile This abandoned vehicle provided Blackhill children with their entertainment in January 1969, despite the obvious dangers

► Constructive This youngster clearly had a great time operating his Meccano bridge in 1971

▲ Worth the wait
Holidaymakers queue in Glasgow Central Station during July, 1966, for the trains that will take them to the seaside

◄ Full to capacity
This Clyde steamer was leaving from Bridge Wharf in 1948 to head 'doon the watter' with more than 2000 passengers on board

▲ **Lunchtime concert** These were popular in George Square in the 1940s and took place directly outside the City Chambers. Performing on this occasion was the band of the Prince of Wales Dragoon Guards

▶ **Entertainment**
The Creole skiffle group played a unique gig on a Central Station platform in November, 1957. No doubt many of the passengers on the train were impressed

Motorcade
Thirty members of the Quickly Club gather outside Andy McNeil's shop in 1956. They were about to set off on their first run from Langlands Road to Houston

▲ **Tough times** This family stand outside a bookmaker's shop in the Gorbals in 1969, no doubt hoping for some good news from inside the premises

▼ **Follow the watercart** Scotstoun Showground was the venue for Hyndland Secondary School's annual sports day in 1939. It must have been a really hot day

▲ **Traffic jam?** No, it was a 'conga line' of 120 big-hearted Glasgow taxi drivers heading from Mearnskirk Hospital, in East Renfrewshire, to Troon on their annual – and much-loved – outing to the seaside. It's a tradition that has stood the test of time and has been enjoyed by thousands of children down the years

Mean streets Living conditions were poor but residents in this Blackhill street, pictured in 1966, finally got their way and the slums were torn down

▲ **Stop, driver** This double decker bus was converted into a playhouse for children in the Arden area of the city – and they all look delighted with their new play area

Improvisation Who needs an expensive boat when you have a tin bath, oars – and a fertile imagination? These 1966 Gorbals kids knew how to enjoy themselves

Impressive The Daily Record and Sunday Mail 'stall' at the 1938 Empire Exhibition, which was held at Bellahouston Park

First with the news – even in 1938!

The Empire Exhibition was just one of the many high-profile events staged in 20th century Glasgow

▲ **Crowning glory** The Glasgow University Charities Queen takes a lap of honour in her horse and carriage at Ibrox Stadium in 1949

▶ **Great fun** Visitors have a go at the water slide during the 1901 Glasgow International Exhibition, which was staged to showcase the city's excellence in art, science and industry

Serene
A beautiful evening in Alexandra Park, Dennistoun. The park was named after Princess Alexandra of Denmark and was opened in 1870

IT'S NO SECRET that Glaswegians love a good night out. Equally, if there's an opportunity to spend an afternoon with the family in one of our many parks, it's grabbed with both hands.

And that's just one of the many contradictions this great city has always featured, a place where grimy tenements stood shoulder to shoulder with well-tended parks. In fact, it's our surfeit of lush outside space that has helped Glasgow earn its Dear Green Place moniker.

Glasgow is a people place and, from the days of the Great Exhibition to the Pope's visit and the thousands of folk who regularly take part in the city's charity races, we love any old excuse to get out and about.

The Glasgow Garden Festival of 1988 was right up there with

Winter wonderland The ice has well and truly taken hold in Rouken Glen Park in 1931 and the beautiful waterfall is in danger of freezing over

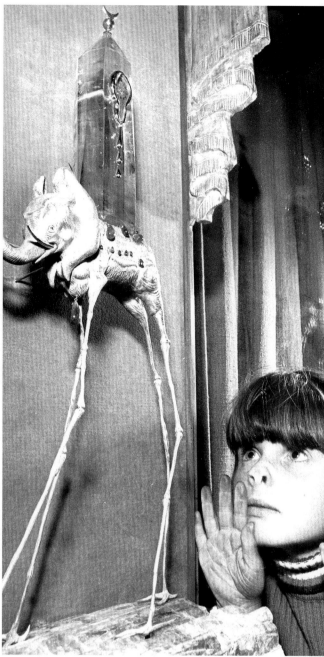

▲ **Closer look** Little Karen McCapra gets a close up of an Elephant at the hugely successful 'Art in Jewels' exhibition at Glasgow Art Gallery and Museum in 1973

Whether it's a big event, a day in the park, or just a great night out, you'll find Glaswegians are always up for it

the many other exhibitions and festivals held in this special corner of the world. We had dignitaries galore, including Prince Charles and Princess Diana, visit the festival.

And many bravely took their seats on the never-to-be-forgotten, white-knuckle, Coca-Cola ride, which thrilled thousands and was apparently responsible for the removal of hundreds of sets of false teeth!

Some of the greatest musical acts of our time, such as the legendary Frank Sinatra and pop princess Kylie Minogue, have made their way to Glasgow, where audiences have often been described as the "most passionate around".

But it is strange to think that evangelist Billy Graham attracted more punters to Hampden than the Rolling Stones. That's the beauty of a city that makes up the rules as it goes along. There's nothing stereotypical about Glasgow.

One week, former Labour Prime Minister Michael Foot packs 'em in at Queen's Park for an important political rally, next, we're peering up at our Glasgow's Smiles Better campaign.

▲ **Look and learn** Victor Kennedy, 77, shows a youngster how to play with a gird and cleek (bowling hoop) in Linn Park, Castlemilk

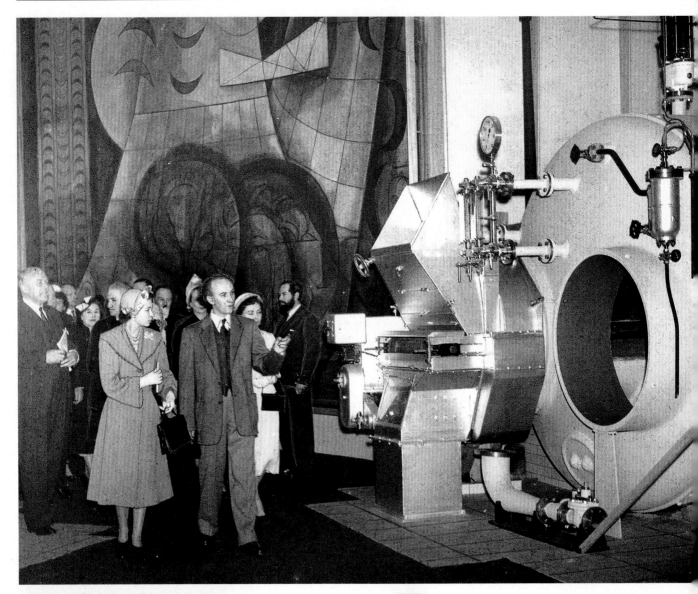

▲ **Royal visit** Princess Elizabeth has a look around the steam section at the Industrial Power Exhibition of May, 1951, a year before she became Queen

Spreading the word This pretty evangelist, accompanied by an accordionist, sings at a Sunday afternoon rally

▲ **Gleam machine** This sparkling Riley car was taking part i the famous Monte Carlo rally and stopped off in Glasgow fo quick snap outside the Central Hotel

▶ **Charismatic** Famous evangelist Billy Graham speaks to students at Glasgow Technical College during a Scottish 'crusade' in April, 1955

Celebration
Residents of Rolland Street, in Maryhill, have a party to commemorate the coronation of Queen Elizabeth in June, 1953

Beauty and the Marines The Sauchiehall Street Festival finished up with a parade of beauty queens and members of the Royal Marines

▲ **Bitter protest** This anti-Poll Tax parade was one of many that took place in Glasgow

▲ **Doing a jig** Youngsters dance the Sailor's Hornpipe at a Highland dance competition held in the city in July, 1955

Main attraction Massive crowds flocked to the impressive 1938 Empire Exhibition held at Bellahouston Park, on the south side of the city

▲ **White-knuckle ride** One of the most popular attractions at the 1988 Glasgow Garden Festival was the Coca-Cola Roller. It proved that many Glaswegians love a good scare

◀ **Top team** A publicity shot for the Glasgow Scouts Gang Show, 1967. It was taken outside the old Alhambra Theatre on the corner of Waterloo Street and Wellington Street

▲ **By the right, quick march** The Boys Brigade have long been a popular fixture and fitting of Glasgow life. This well-attended parade was organised to mark the centenary of the organisation in 1986

House call Controversial MP Enoch Powell, right, travelled up to the Red Road flats, in the north of the city, in 1969 to lend a hand to the prospective Conservative candidate. Powell was Minister for Health at the time

When tenements gave way to high-rise flats

Glaswegians were certainly moving up in the world when city fathers decided to clear slum tenement blocks

GLASGOW Frame by Frame

Public bath A Govan mum gets ready to wash her kids in the sink. This was one of many Glasgow flats which did not have a bathroom

Fancy a pint? A 1967 view of the Victoria Bar, on Victoria Road. There was a pub on almost every corner in Glasgow at one time

IF AN ENGLISHMAN'S home is his castle then a Glaswegian's was surely his tenement flat. It may not have provided a life of Riley for inner-city dwellers but there's no denying that living at such close quarters would have helped foster and develop a real sense of community among neighbours.

Living on top of one another meant there was nothing else for it but to get on, although no doubt many an argument ensued over whose turn it was to wash the communal stairs.

But peering at some of our images of early tenement life illustrates just how tough it must have been throughout large parts of the 20th century. Rat-catching was a favourite pastime of kids growing up in many areas as the less-than-friendly furries regularly burrowed their way into people's homes.

Disease was rife, although playing in the wastelands of early 20th century Glasgow would definitely have helped give a welcome boost to the immune system.

Squatting became a necessity for some, as rent increases priced them out of legitimately living in a privately-owned property.

And then our city fathers came up with the answer to overcrowding – high-rise flats. Early models were based on French examples and one of Glasgow's first developments, the Red Road flats, in the north of the city, went up in 1966. England got the World Cup and we were offered sky-high living.

Slum tenements in some of Glasgow's poorest areas were bulldozed to make way for these enormous 29 and 31-storey flats, which, it was promised, would improve the quality of living for so many folk.

And there's no doubt it did, until tales of anti-social behaviour and broken lifts meant people were akin to prisoners in their own homes.

Housing in Glasgow has once again cranked up a notch thanks to the many waterside developments that are providing people with a style of living never before witnessed in the city.

Glasgow has certainly moved on from the days of slum tenement dwelling.

▲ Race for life This youngster, photographed outside a tenement block in Govan in 1956, is clearly in a rush to get home – probably for his dinner

▲ **Shadowland** The Govan end of Copland Road, with the dock in the background, in 1948

▲ **The 66 steps** Yes, they were counted in 1936! The steps lead from Queen Margaret Drive to Wilton Street and Kelvinside Gardens in the north-west of the city

◢ **A 'Posh' street** Dudley Drive, in Hyndland, in 1958

▲ **Back courts** The gardens in Hill Street, Garnethill, looked out on to Renfrew Street in the 1950s

▲ **This old house** Provand's Lordship is the city's oldest house. It was built in 1471 as part of St Nicholas' Hospital by the Bishop of Glasgow and stands in the shadow of Glasgow Cathedral

▲ **Closed for business** There weren't many shops left open in the Blackhill area of the city when this snap was taken in 1970

▲ **Grim past** The oldest thatched house in Glasgow sat at the corner of Ladywell Street and Duke Street – and at one time it was occupied by the hangman

One step at a time This unfortunate squatter and his family moved into a flat in Nitshill that flooded in 1949. It's no wonder they look forlorn

▶ **Gentility** A charming row of terraced houses in Great Western Road in 1948

▼ **Cobbled streets** These were the norm throughout Glasgow, as this picture taken around 1948 shows, until the council ripped up surfaces all over the city and replaced them with tarmac

▼ **Busy Glasgow** A lively scene from Renfield Street in 1964. Note the popular Lauder's pub at the corner of Sauchiehall Street

◀ **Heartbreaking**
It's Christmas, 1947, and a group of 30 women and children enjoy a complimentary dinner before having to return to the Forresthall Institution, a city hostel for the poor

▲ **Leafy suburb** Clayton Terrace, in Dennistoun, looks every inch the desirable location in this 1946 photograph

▲ **Worldly possessions**
A group of squatters deliver their furniture to a prospective flat near the city's Barlinnie Prison in 1946

▶ **Falling down**
A bulldozed tenement block in Maryhill in March, 1975

When jobs were in plentiful supply

There was a time when apprenticeships were easy to come by and no one ever feared being out of work in the city

Bright spark
Apprentice John Berwick trains as an electric welder at Glasgow's Stow College in 1946

IN THE EARLY 1900s, Glasgow was viewed as one of the UK's leading centres for trade and manufacturing. There was the proverbial "job for life" and the 1901 International Exhibition merely cemented our place as one of the country's most marketable cities.

Just as sons tended to be named after dads or granddads, so too did they follow in their footsteps down the pit or into an apprenticeship on Clydeside. It was the family way.

Greta Moore left Whitehill Secondary School, in Glasgow's Dennistoun, at 15, and had more than a dozen jobs by the time she had celebrated her 19th birthday.

"That's the way it was back then. I worked in a city centre steak house, pubs and as a clippie (conductress) on the Glasgow trams before I was 20," she said. "I was never once idle when I was younger, even though I didn't do particularly well at school."

May Tran was also just 15 when she was given a start in her local branch of Henry Healy's grocers on Maryhill Road. She said: "I wanted to be a window dresser but the counter job tided me over until I could get to college to learn dressing. It was all about who you knew back then."

Due to a plentiful supply of jobs, most folk tended to work no more than a mile or two from home, which was true of Stephen Hannigan, a native of Anderston.

But his chosen trade led him down a dead-end path. He completed a four-year apprenticeship as an armature winder at a city centre firm. A "winder" repaired and reconditioned coils for electric motors.

Stephen said: "Turned out it was a trade that offered very few job prospects. I knew someone who had been a winder and that's why I took it on. That was 40 years ago and I haven't been back on the tools since."

Many youngsters took on apprenticeships at one of the big shipyards on the Clyde, but jobs have since dwindled dramatically at the yards and teenagers are more likely to be found working in call centres these days than in heavy industry. A true sign of the times.

First class Postman James Taylor demonstrates the new Pedestrian Controlled Electric Trolley in 1967

A dog's life The Glasgow Vet School in 1930, when well-known author James Herriot was a student there

Gigantic Crane driver John Currie high above the biggest ship ever built on the River Clyde. This picture of the oil tanker Naess Scotsman was taken back in 1973

▶ **Ready for work**
The famed Glasgow Boy Messengers of the Post Office pictured during the 1930s

▼ **Carpetbaggers**
These 1963 prisoners at Barlinnie were hard at it in the rug-making shop

▼ **Clocking in** Alarm clock assembly at Westclox in November, 1949

▲ **Looking good** Air stewardesses from British Caledonian model new outfits in 1964 and, right, an aircraft on the tarmac

SATURDAY
8 AM – 1 PM

▼ **All systems slow** Bustling Glasgow Central Station was even more packed than usual after commuters were delayed by rail workers' industrial action

◄ **Freshest in town** Bessie Swan was a regular flower seller in Sauchiehall Street in the 1950s

▲ **A place in the sun**
Women office workers
take advantage of the
summer sunshine in
George Square

▶ **Dying art** The
Lawrie Brothers hard
at work during the
1920s in their shed
making a dinghy from
compressed wood
fibres

Time out Two drivers sit and chat on the steps of a tram during a terminus stop

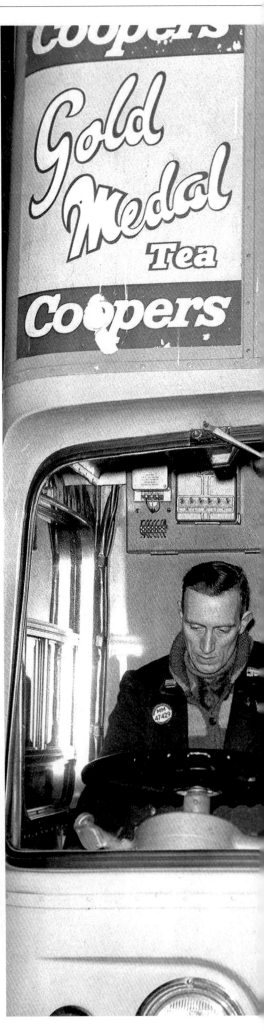

▼ **A picture of concentration** Bagpipe maker William Connell at a workshop in Yoker in 1954

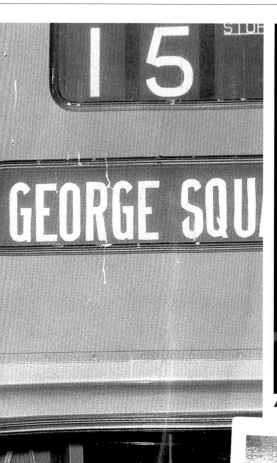

▲ **Stand well back** Passengers wait for their morning train at Glasgow Queen Street station

◄ **All aboard**
The Finnieston passenger ferry crosses the River Clyde in 1953

City-bound
A bus driver gets ready to begin his journey – headed for George Square

▲ **Initiation ceremony** Newly qualified cooperman Willie Morgan gets covered in bucketfuls of rubbish from workmates after finishing his apprenticeship in a Glasgow factory

Neigh bother
In the 1950s, workhorses were used by shipbuilders to transport wooden scaffolding rigs

Shipbuilding was a Clydeside art

Believe it or not, but there was a time when Glasgow was at the centre of the industrial universe

World-famous
Shipyards on the Clyde, such
as these pictured in the 1950s,
had a reputation for turning
out the finest vessels

THE industrial might
of Glasgow has left an
indelible mark on every
corner of the globe.

From the construction of our
first-class trains to the ships that
still sail the world's waters, Glasgow
played its part.

The growth of the industrial
revolution, at the turn of the 19th
and 20th centuries, changed our
landscape forever.

The population and economy of
Glasgow had expanded to such an
extent that the city became one of
the world's pre-eminent centres of
heavy engineering.

There was a jobs boom like never
before. Men flocked from far and
wide to take up positions in one of
the new factories or shipyards.

At its peak in the 1930s, Glasgow's
population grew to an all-time high
of more than 1.1million – making
it the fourth largest city in Europe
behind London, Paris and Berlin.

What was once a rural settlement
had developed into the second

The Clyde was at the centre of a huge jobs boom that transformed Glasgow into the second city of the Empire

city of the Empire. Glasgow was
now firmly on the map – and it
continued to grow.

It was the area along the River
Clyde that provided thousands of
jobs. Shipyards such as Beardmore's,
Fairfield's, John Brown's and
Yarrow's became world famous
for turning out the most beautiful
of vessels.

In the 1940s, the Bruce Plan was
introduced to decrease housing
density. It also proposed the
building of several industrial estates.

In 1946, the New Towns Scotland

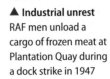

▲ **Industrial unrest**
RAF men unload a
cargo of frozen meat at
Plantation Quay during
a dock strike in 1947

Act started a mass exodus to
outlying, purpose-built communiti
such as East Kilbride, Castlemilk
and Drumchapel.

The Clyde Tunnel opened in the
early 1960s and a highway plan wa
set out for a complete restructurin
of our road network. In 1970, wor
started on the Kingston Bridge.

All the projects provided jobs
in the construction sector, while
improving the look of a tired and
grubby city.

It was a win-win situation for
all concerned.

▼ **Heavy work**
Shipyard workers weld
steel plates together

▼ **Vital crossing service**
Renfrew ferry on a slipway on the Clyde in 1956

▲ **Mobile phone** A shipping official uses a walkie-talkie to communicate with
colleagues ahead of the launch of the cargo liner Glenogle from Fairfield's
shipyard in Govan in May, 1962

All smiles No doubt
these Govan shipyard
workers are either going
for their tea or it's a Friday
and it's finishing time!

Fair wages for all That's all these workers were asking for when they gathered in George Square in 1953 to protest at low pay rates

Worrying times Rolls Royce workers voted to strike in November 1955 after a meeting at St Andrew's Hall

▼ **Production line** Workers at Glasgow confectioners Macmillan & Monro wrap Easter eggs in foil. The firm turned out 3000 20oz eggs to satisfy the many sweet tooths in the cit

▲ **Nuts and bolts** Apprentices work on an old car at the Southern Junior Instruction Centre in Kinning Park in 1938. It was the city's number one mechanics shop for apprentices

▲ **One out, all out**
Engineers gather at
Glasgow Green in 1953 to
hear trade union leaders
talk about strike action

Innovation Bosses
from John Brown's Shipyard
gather at Maryhill in 1963
to watch an experiment
involving a new model tank

No v-room for any more!
The Glasgow car market auction of 1969 had more than a few shiny vehicles up for sale

▼ **End of an era** A mechanical digger rips up old tram lines in the city in 1954

▶ **Flip for it**
Workman Willie Duffy gives Albany Hotel chef Frank Boggie a run for his money tossing pancakes on Shrove Tuesday in 1982

City architecture is a real winner

Take a stroll around Glasgow city centre and marvel at our fine buildings, but remember – always look up!

Meeting place
The Tolbooth at Glasgow Cross is a famous landmark and was a centre of commerce. A Beattie's Bread van is in the foreground, on a delivery run

EVERY CITY has its iconic structures. Liverpool has the Royal Liver Building, Manchester its impressive cathedral, while the Joseph Chamberlain Memorial Clock Tower dominates Birmingham – but where do we start with Glasgow?

Our Dear Green Place has always had so much more to offer than the parochial No Mean City label it "earned" from its tough and uncompromising gangland days.

The Old Tolbooth at Glasgow Cross is situated in the heart of the old town centre – once known as Mercat Cross – and dates back to at least the mid-1400s.

As far as landmarks go, it is as good a place as any to start.

Thankfully, the Old Tolbooth is anything but alone in a city where countless statues, fountains and clock towers dominate the skyline.

Throw in some of the most impressive city centre streets in the United Kingdom and you have a city that has more to offer than most.

It's Glasgow's individuality that makes it stand out from the crowd.

The influence of famous architect Charles Rennie Mackintosh can be seen at various locations – most notably the Willow Tea Rooms, Scotland Street School and Queen's Cross Church in Maryhill.

Mackintosh was born in Glasgow in 1868, the fourth of 12 children, and attended Allan Glen's Institution.

He served his apprenticeship with Honeyman & Keppie architectural practice and the first job he worked on was the Glasgow Herald building in Mitchell Lane in 1899.

He was a proponent of the Art Noveau movement and had a considerable influence on European design.

But Mackintosh was in good company, as Alexander "Greek" Thomson also took great pride in helping transform the city into something special.

Thomson's legacy includes Caledonia Road Church in the Gorbals and Cathcart's Holmwood House. He is also credited as having influenced famous New York architect Frank Lloyd Wright.

But there were others who contributed enormously to

▲ Motor city
Motor Union Chambers in Royal Exchange Square in 1920

Glasgow's architectural landscape, too. And the city has so many stunning buildings that it is easy to miss some gems.

One piece of advice often given to visitors is to always "look upwards". It's the best way to see all the little nooks, crannies and idiosyncrasies that the city centre, in particular, is famed for.

In the east of the city, the heavy Victorian influence is replaced by a worthy substitute.

The Moorish Templeton's Carpet Factory was designed to resemble the Gothic-style Doge's Palace in Venice.

When it comes to architecture, Glasgow truly is miles better.

◀ **Long life** The neoclassical Royal Exchange building, built in 1778 as a townhouse for a tobacco lord, became the Gallery of Modern Art in 1996

Flag day
oots the chemist Argyle Street in 948. The corner as a popular eeting place

Victorian splendour An aerial view of Glasgow Cathedral and the Royal Infirmary

◀ **Cityscape** A 1930 view of Victoria Circus and Great Western Road

Hive of activity A typical scene at Glasgow Cross, taken in 1962

Imposing
The Central Hotel stands proudly as traffic makes its way up and down Hope Street and into Gordon Street

▶ **Spaghetti junction**
The Kingston Bridge, now an integral part of the M8 motorway

▲ **Under construction** But the glass-topped St Enoch Centre is almost finished

Mind that tram Busy St Vincent Street in 1949 – complete with cobbled surfaces

▲ **Trading places** The Stock Exchange takes centre stage in this picture of a busy Buchanan Street taken in 1964

▶ **Let's dance** The famous Locarno Ballroom in Sauchiehall Street

▶ **Room for the night** Former Beresford Hotel in Sauchiehall Street, described as Glasgow's first skyscraper, taken from Elmbank Street

▲ Hustle and bustle
Argyle Street in the
1930s, with a flat
up for rent

▶ Georgian elegance
The Grosvenor Hotel,
on Great Western Road
in the west end, in 1931

▶ Fancy a cuppa?
Peacock's tea room and
restaurant in Union Street,
pictured in 1947, was a
popular pit-stop

▶ **Vintage cars** Shawlands Cross, looking towards Kilmarnock Road, in 1951

▲ **Mansion home** Garscube House, on the banks of the River Kelvin in the north of the city, in 1928. It was demolished in 1957

Hidden landmark The St Mungo's Well and Fountain in a back court off the Gallowgate, near to the famous Saracen's Head pub

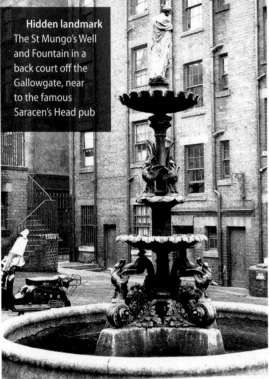

▶ **Standing proud** Battlefield Monument, in the south side of the city, in 1956

▼ **Victorian architecture** Bridgeton Working Men's Club

▲ **Halcyon days** The Art Deco-influenced Kelvin Hall in 1929

▲ **Baby boom** The Royal Maternity Hospital at Rottenrow in 1969

Fighting war on the home front

Glaswegians coped stoically with the perils of war and the constant threat of bombing from Hitler's Luftwaffe

False alarm
The Home Guard carry out a training exercise in 1941, simulating an attack on a Glasgow railway station

THE WRITING was on the wall for the residents of our city when the might of Hitler's aerial war machine dropped bomb after bomb upon London during a constant two-hour blitz in September, 1940.

And while it would be another six months before the Luftwaffe turned their attention to Glasgow, our citizens knew it was only a matter of time before strategic points north of Hadrian's Wall became top targets on German radar.

When it arrived, the relentless bombing campaign was designed to demoralise spirits but it had the opposite effect, and a nation under constant bombardment was quickly galvanised.

As each night fell, the haunting sound of air-raid sirens would fill neighbourhoods already on edge with dread and fear, and everyone would quickly make for their nearest cover, whether a purpose-built Anderson shelter or a makeshift refuge at an underground station.

So much of Glasgow was destroyed by the bombing and while Clydebank, on the outskirts of the city, bore the brunt of Hitler's fury, areas such as Kilmun Street, in Maryhill, were also badly affected, with row upon row of tenement buildings razed to the ground in ruthless fashion.

World War II lasted six years, so the threat of bombing became the norm and Glaswegians were constantly preparing for the possibility of attack.

Children had regular drills at school in which they donned gas masks and rehearsed leaving the premises in a safe and orderly manner.

Thousands more children were evacuated to potentially safer locations throughout Great Britain and it would be many long months before they would be reunited again with distressed parents. It was a dreadful time for all concerned.

Women stepped up to the plate and began to take on jobs normally undertaken by menfolk, of whom thousands were on the continent fighting against the might of the Nazis.

Rationing became a way of life and each adult was presented with a little brown ration book, which set out guidelines of what they were allowed each week.

Items such as milk, eggs and bread were exceedingly scarce and all perishable goods were treated with great importance in the home. Heaven forbid one of the children should sneakily gulp down a big drink of milk!

Glasgow's Home Guard was operational from 1940 to 1944 and played its part in retaining order and a degree of normality while battle raged all around Europe and North Africa.

It was a welcome sight when soldiers finally returned home at the end of the long and bloody conflict, although, for many, there would be no such celebratory homecomings.

▼ Proud moment
A victory parade was organised to mark our success in finally defeating Germany in World War I. The picture was taken in George Square in 1918

Precaution
An Army despatch rider in August of 1941 with his gas mask on. Glaswegians were asked to carry their masks with them at all times

▲ **Packed stadium** Glasgow Police march around Hampden Park in 1939 – carrying their gas masks

▲ **Parade** The Stock Exchange Corps line up in Buchanan Street during World War I

◀ **Exercise** Members of the Home Guard don gas masks in August, 1941

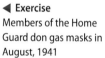

Essential kit One lady carries her gas mask in its box in September, 1939. The Government was concerned that Hitler would carry out a chemical attack on Britain

◀ **Victory parade** Citizens packed out George Square to greet the news that World War I was over

▲ **All smiles** But these kids were off to a Government evacuation camp at Abington, Lanarkshire, in 1940

Heroic effort
Sailors on leave pull wreckage from a Clydeside building which had been bombed in an air raid

AIR RAID SHELTER

SHELTER

SAVINGS ON MAIN HALL

HASTEN THE DAY

NATIONAL WAR BONDS

▲ **Safe and sound**
A warden secures the door of an air raid shelter in George Square in 1940

▲ **Devastation** A tram lies destroyed and a fire precaution officer sounds his whistle in the wake of another terrifying air raid by the German Luftwaffe in Clydebank in March 1941

▼ **Devastation** Rescuers search a building in Kent Street during a World War II bombing raid

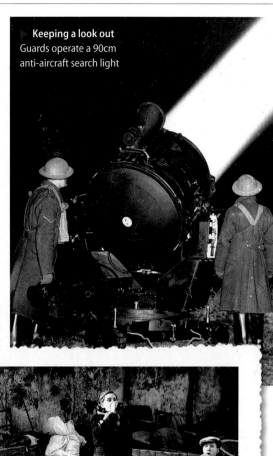

Keeping a look out Guards operate a 90cm anti-aircraft search light

▲ **Open house** Survivors of the blitz on Clydeside in March 1941 set up home in a ruined house

Hero A fireman rescues a little girl from a Clydebank street during the blitz of 1941

Homecoming
Queen Street station is packed as crowds welcome servicemen home on leave in January, 1945

Hero's welcome
On-leave Robert Martin, from Glasgow, at Edinburgh Waverley station in 1945

▲ **Fire power**
Crowds perch on top of an air raid shelter to get a glimpse of a New Covenanter tank in George Square in 1941

◄ **Child's play**
Evacuated children play with toys at a temporary home in September, 1939

◄ **Victory smiles**
Wrens and sailors celebrate VE Day near the end of World War II in 1945

▲ **Street party** Residents of Ferguson Street prepare for the homecoming of a local hero, soldier Jimmie McGuire, who had spent four years in the Middle East

▲ **Back in stock**
With World War II at an end, these ladies were delighted to visit a store in the west end of Glasgow and find that new stocks of nylon had been delivered

March past
The end of World War II was celebrated in style, with a victory parade through George Square

Glasgow gun siege
A policeman carrying his cap runs along Great Western Road while other cops watch from behind cars in July, 1969. The officers were on the trail of murder suspect James Griffiths in Holyrood Crescent

Tarred with the No Mean City brush

Glasgow has a rich cultural and social heritage – but with a dark underbelly of gangs and violence

GLASGOW has had its fair share of gangs down the years.

When the Potato Famine hit Ireland in 1845, almost a quarter of its population headed for pastures new, Glasgow included, and the city's gang landscape changed forever.

Ghettos sprung up around the city, which proved a fertile breeding ground for gangs as Irishmen looked to protect their own against attacks from Glaswegians.

Nowhere was this more evident than in the Partick area, where some of the fiercest battles took place on Dumbarton Road.

From that moment on, battle

Battles between gangsters bring fear to the streets and give the city an unwelcome reputation

lines were drawn and territory became all-important.

By the 1930s, Glasgow was likened to Chicago, as the razor gangs ruled the roost.

The city became notorious throughout the rest of the UK as a hotbed of gang violence.

"Johnnie Stark", from the Gorbals, was immortalised in the dark novel, No Mean City.

In July 1969, violence spilled out on to the streets when cops

arrived at a flat in Holyrood Crescent to question murder suspect James Griffiths.

He fled, pursued by police and went on a gun rampage, wounding 13 people before eventually being shot.

Griffiths became the first wanted man on record to be shot dead by Scottish cops.

But it wasn't just hoodlums and gangsters who kept our emergency services busy.

March 28, 1960, will be remembered as the night 19 firemen lost their lives during a blaze at the Cheapside Street whisky bond.

The warehouse contained a million gallons of whisky and 450 firemen fought the blaze. It was Britain's worst-ever peacetime fire services disaster.

Terrible tragedy
Twenty-two workers at a Glasgow warehouse lost their lives in the James Watt Street fire, in 1968, after being trapped in premises with barred windows

▲ **Warehouse fire**
An upholstery factory in James Watt Street was destroyed by a massive blaze in November, 1968

Heroes Firemen from Anderston were commended for their bravery fighting the Cheapside Street fire

▲ **Working overtime** This fire engine had been in operation day and night to fight the flames from the Cheapside Street whisky bond blaze in 1960

▲ **Reaching up** Fire ripped through the top part of the Central Hotel building in 1951 – and the clock tower suffered the worst damage. Hope Street was closed temporarily as a result

▲ **Fatality** The Glasgow gun siege of 1969 ended with the body of James Griffiths being taken away by ambulance staff

Peace talks
Crooner Frankie Vaughan visited Easterhouse in the 1960s in an attempt to persuade gangs to down tools. Here, Frankie speaks with gang members

▲ Horror scene
Margaret Barton and her two children were killed in Govanhill Street in July, 1958. Her husband, Stanley, was later charged with their murder

▲ Run for cover People flee as a major gang fight takes place in Tollcross Road, Parkhead, in 1933

▼ **Romantic** Members of the Blue Angels motorcycle gang attend a wedding in 1971

▼ **Show trial** Those 'responsible' for the Glasgow riots of 1919 appear in the dock. They included Manny Shinwell, a great trade union leader of the early 20th century

Weapons amnesty Children in Easterhouse look on in amazement in 1968 at the array of deadly weapons that were handed in

▲ **Trouble** A police officer attends an incident in which several shop windows were smashed in the Saltmarket in 1931

▲ **Cuffed** Convicted killer Peter Manuel is led into Barlinnie. The murderer hanged in 1958

▲ **Appeal** A detective puts up a poster in the hope of catching infamous Glasgow killer Bible John. The man in the photofit is thought to have murdered three women between 1968 and 1969

▲ **Grisly** The infamous bath in which Dr Buck Ruxton murdered two women in 1935 is taken to the Forensic Medicine University in Glasgow for tests

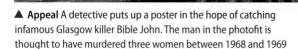

Innocent William Watt, accused of murder in 1956, is taken to Glasgow Sheriff Court to face trial. He was later cleared of murder and Peter Manuel was convicted

▲ **Infamous Gangster** Arthur Thompson Snr is pictured, cent with high-flying lawyers Nicholas Fairbairn and Joe Beltrami

Everyone loved a good night out

From dance halls to the theatre and the pictures, Glasgow night life had something for everyone

In the mood Big-name bands regularly performed at Green's Playhouse dance hall in Glasgow. In this 1950s snap, the crowd are enjoying the sound of the big band

GLASGOW'S theatreland might not hold as much sway as London's famed West End but when it came to theatrical grounding, there was no crowd tougher than the audience at the Glasgow Empire.

Situated in Sauchiehall Street – on the site of the current Dino's restaurant – they called it the "comedian's graveyard" and it toughened up the occasional southern softy.

In the 20th century, the city was awash with theatres and Glaswegians looked upon a night out at the Alhambra, Pavilion or Metropole as their main source of entertainment.

But we also loved to dance and there were equally as many dance halls where teenagers would go in search of a "lumber" or simply to show off their dancing skills.

Strictly Come Dancing may have re-introduced the art to the masses but the "jiggin" was always in vogue in Glasgow throughout the whole of the 1900s.

Most areas of the city housed provincial dance halls. The Dennistoun Palais was right up there with the very best, while the Cameo in Shawlands and The Roxy in Maryhill also packed them in at weekends.

Later on, many dance halls closed but re-invented themselves in time to cash in on a new craze that was sweeping the city – bingo.

This form of entertainment was certainly not restricted to weekends, as people played – and still play – seven days a week in halls the length and breadth of the city.

Cinema was also a popular form of entertainment and the city centre hosted some fine picture houses. The Odeon, in Renfield Street, was arguably the best known, although the ABC in Sauchiehall Street gave it a real run for its money.

Provincial cinemas included the Astoria, in Possil Road, the Seamore and the Blythswood, in Maryhill, the Aldwych, in Paisley Road West, the Dalmarnock Picture House, in Nuneaton Street, and the Lyceum, in Govan.

Nowadays, Glaswegians have a world of entertainment at their fingertips.

And the times when children stamped their feet during a matinee performance of a cowboy and Indian film to get the lights "put up" are a dim and distant memory.

▼ **Lengthy wait**
Fans of American singer Johnny Ray wait for him to appear from the stage door after a concert at the Glasgow Empire

▼ **Balancing act** Alma Michaels' dog, Susie, was a star turn at the Kelvin Hall circus in December, 1957

Cooling down
Rolling Stones frontman Mick Jagger throws a bucket of water over himself during a gig at the Apollo in 1976

Tonic Child patients at Mearnskirk Hospital are entertained by Barrowland resident band, The Gaybirds

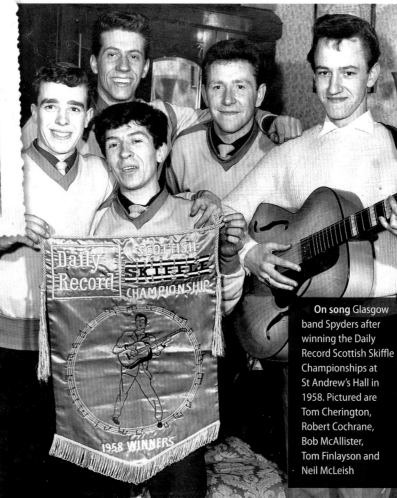

On song Glasgow band Spyders after winning the Daily Record Scottish Skiffle Championships at St Andrew's Hall in 1958. Pictured are Tom Cherington, Robert Cochrane, Bob McAllister, Tom Finlayson and Neil McLeish

▼ **Star attraction** Double act Grace Clark and Colin Murray top the bill at the Metropole Theatre in Stockwell Street

▶ **Twist and shout** Teenagers dance the night away at the opening of Scotland's first Beatles fan club in Bath Street.

Eyes down
The Palace bingo hall was a favourite haunt for Gorbals women in 1968 – and a handful of men! The Citizens' Theatre was just next door

▲ **Unforgettable** Crowds flocked to the Empire Theatre in 1952 to see the spectacular panto Robinson Crusoe On Ice

▼ **Come dancing** Socialite Farquhar MacRae and his wife Alice are among dancers at the Locarno Ballroom in 1923

Take your partners
The Reggie Harkins Formation Team perform at Daily Record Scottish Open Dance Championships at the Locarno Ballroom in 1962

▲ **Perfect feet** Ballroom dancing in Glasgow – 1964-style!

Just champion
George Stewart and Elma McNicol take to the floor at the 1962 Amateur Dance Championships – and show us the cha-cha

▲ **Sports bar** The Tall Cranes, Govan, is packed as football fans watch the 1967 England v Scotland match at Wembley on a big screen via a projector. Scotland won 3-2

Live advertising Model Anne Milligan helps promote the movie Cleopatra at the Curzon cinema in Sauchiehall Street in 1963 by lying in a glass case dressed as the Egyptian icon

Entertainment centre The Curzon cinema stood proudly next to the Locarno Ballroom in Sauchiehall Street

▶ **A night at the opera** Thomas Lawlor, left, and Iwan Raikes on stage at the King's Theatre in 1969 in Gilbert and Sullivan's HMS Pinafore

▼ **Playtime** Schoolgirls aged between eight and 12 receive lessons in dressmaking at a shop in Sauchiehall Street in 1955. They received two lessons each week during the school holidays

▼ **In the picture** The Vogue cinema, Knightswood, in 1957, three years before it was demolished

▼ **Image change** Model Fiona Best shows off the Mr Men-style logo at the launch of Glasgow's 'Miles Better' campaign in George Square in 1983

▲ **Read all about it** Children from St Scholastica's Primary, Easterhouse, promote National Book Week on a fun bus

Patter capital
A salesman at the Barras in
1972 talks Glasgow 'wifeys'
into purchasing his wares

Glaswegians shopped 'til they dropped

Despite money being tight, people were never short of stores or markets in which to spend their hard-earned cash

▲ **It's all go** The junction of Buchanan Street and St Enoch Square in March, 1945, with a horse and cart taking centre stage

I REMEMBER when Glasgow was the shopping capital of the world – or so it seemed. The city centre was awash with quality department stores such as Lewis's, Wood & Selby's and Arnott's. All long gone, but all shops that evoke great memories in Glaswegians of a certain vintage.

If you had an extra few quid in your wallet, you could nip into Goldberg's, in the old Merchant City. In fact, who could forget the corny television advert, with the chauffeur in the lead role… "Jeffrey, take me to Goldberg's" went the catchy jingle, and many folk did just that.

In fact, Goldberg's was one of the first stores in the city centre to offer personal accounts to shoppers. Others were happy to accept Provident cheques on which many families relied.

Shops such as Woolworths, Wylie & Lochhead and Grandfare also packed them in on a Saturday afternoon, although it wasn't just the centre of Glasgow that enjoyed

swarming hordes of weekend shoppers.

Further east, the "Barras" had them flocking in their thousands. It was open Saturdays and Sundays – like the present time – but back then there was definitely something magical about the area surrounding the old Barrowlands dance hall.

Market traders set up their stalls early on a Saturday morning and you could buy just about anything you wanted. Secondhand goods, toys, clothing, bric-a-brac and, of course, curtains and fresh meat.

An odd combination, I know, but the banter was exceptional and I'm convinced that housewives just purchased a pair of net curtains and six gigot chops because the chat was so good.

Mobile shops were also popular when many Glaswegians "emigrated" to the new towns, while much closer to home, people listened out for the vans in many of the large housing schemes such as Drumchapel and Easterhouse.

▲ **Treat** There were many items under a penny that children could buy in a sweet shop back in 1933

Heading into the "town" at the weekend was a ritual, even though pavement space was at a premium. Come Christmas, you could multiply that footfall by a dozen.

The festive season at the Barras was always a real novelty as the market remained open until at least 10pm on Christmas Eve.

But the most popular of all Glasgow "shops" remains … the public bar. Many a wrong has been put to right and many a wallet emptied in the humble boozer, and even though we have witnessed a sharp decline in traditional pubs, many workers have retained the old Scottish mindset of "Let's grab a pint at finishing time".

▲ **In out the rain** This couple are nipping into Craig's Coffee Room, in St Vincent Street, for a cuppa and some respite from the cold and damp weather in February, 1950

▲ **Festive** Christmas lights in Glasgow city centre look spectacular in 1966 – and are still a huge attraction

Everything under one roof Lewis's store in Argyle Street was probably the best-known store in town – and one famous for its Christmas window displays. The Glasgow branch opened in 1929 and survived for almost 70 years

The hustle and the bustle Saturday afternoon shopping in the city centre is a long-held ritual that has been enjoyed by many over the years

▲ **Flag day** The famous Wylie & Lochhead store in Buchanan Street pictured in 1953

▲ **Stocking up** Canny Glaswegians get a sniff of a price rise on whisky during 1968 and form a 50-yard queue outside an off-sales to make sure they still get a dram at a reasonable cost

Come and buy
This gents outfitters took coupons in 1949 in payment for its quality garments

▶ **On the move** Davie's mobile van provided residents of Cranhill with a regular groceries service

Good fit Alice Asposto, daughter of police superintendent Gordon Leith, buys a new pair of shoes in 1957

▼ **Good price** Customers at Grandfare check out the pots and pans sale at the store in March, 1965

That looks nice Two young ladies indulge in a spot of window shopping in Sauchiehall Street back in 1951

▲ **Ah, that's better!** Clementine Wilson, a 22-year-old sales assistant, bathes her feet after working non-stop during a Christmas rush at C&A in the 1960s

There you go Shoppers getting served in Woolworth's, New City Road, in 1958

▼ **Forward thinking** The Kelvin House shop, in Partick, captured in 1955, decided to redesign their store so that their display was given more prominence

Material girls The fabric counter at Lewis's, in Argyle Street, doing a roaring trade in 1947

Taking a peek into Glasgow's future

The city is in great shape and ready to shine brightly as the 2014 Commonwealth Games loom large

Innovative The Clyde Arc, better known as the 'Squinty Bridge', looks fantastic by night. It was opened in 2006 – the first north/south crossing since the Kingston Bridge

SO, WE'VE taken a stroll down memory lane and stirred many a dormant thought in the process. Memories you thought would never emerge again.

Now it's time to see how Glasgow is shaping up at present and what's in store for the future.

And once again, the River Clyde is taking centre stage – with the new Hydro set to be Scotland's new home of live entertainment.

It also adds to the 21st century feel started by the SECC and Clyde Auditorium.

The 100-metre high Science Centre vantage point also gives incredible views over the city and draws comparisons with the Tait Tower, the piece de resistance at the 1938 Empire Exhibition held at Bellahouston Park.

The Science Centre was built on the site of the 1988 Glasgow Garden Festival. The 3000-seater Armadillo

has attracted many big names, and the Britain's Got Talent audition that gave Susan Boyle her big break.

When the Hydro is completed in 2013, it will seat 12,000 and rival the big venues south of the Border.

But, more importantly, it will once again confirm Glasgow as a must-visit destination for top acts.

For years, the Clyde was a hive of activity as ships such as the Queen Elizabeth II slipped into the river. But, after a lengthy lull, the Clyde Waterfront Regeneration has breathed new life into our bonny banks.

Throughout the years, one fixture has remained a constant on the Clyde – the famous Finnieston Crane, our city's iconic landmark.

And we are currently enjoying further regeneration in the east end of Glasgow with the Commonwealth Games set to arrive in these parts in less than two years.

Now you see them
Five of the Mitchellhill multi-storey flats are demolished in 2003

◀ **Coming down** This Gorbals block of flats at Norfolk Court was razed to the ground in 2010 – and was watched by a large group of residents

▶ **Then and now**
The Glasgow Harbour development was once the biggest grain factory in Europe. It was sited at Meadowside, in the west end of town

▷ **Glasgow at night**
The stunning River Clyde shines like a beacon of light as the Finnieston Crane stands proudly behind our own 'Squinty Bridge'

GLASGOW FRAME *by* FRAME

Illuminated
The Glasgow Science Centre looks incredible by night

◄ **Landmark** The Clyde Auditorium, affectionately known as the Armadillo, opened in 1997 and has drawn comparisons with the Sydney Opera House

► **City centre sparkle** Royal Exchange Square, with the Gallery of Modern Art on the right

▲ **Striking** The Commonwealth Arena and Sir Chris Hoy Velodrome are ready for the 2014 Games

◄ **Futuristic** The BT building on the Broomielaw, as photographed in 2000